Lip

For Gus and Liz

Acknowlegements:

Acknowledgements are due to the editors of the following publications in which some of these poems first appeared: *Acumen, The Brighton Book, Dream Catcher, Magma, Poetry London, The North, The Rialto, Smiths Knoll.*

'The Biting Point' was commended in the National Poetry Competition, 2006, and 'Cut' won second prize in the Kent and Sussex Poetry Competition, 2005. 'The Fathers' was commended in the Ware Poets Open Poetry Competition 2006.

Thanks to Sarah Salway, Tammy Yoseloff, Jackie Wills, Clare Best, Lorna Thorpe, Vicky Buckley-Jennings, Kim Lasky, John McCullough and Brendan Cleary for criticism and advice. Particular thanks to Neil Rollinson and Ros Barber for close reading, detailed feedback and heroic patience.

I am very grateful for an Arts Council grant in 2005 which enabled me to work on this book; thanks to Keiren Phelan for his enduring kindness and support.

Lip

Catherine Smith

Smith/Doorstop Books

Published 2007 by
Smith/Doorstop Books
The Poetry Business
The Studio
Byram Arcade
Westgate
Huddersfield HD1 1ND

ISBN 978-1-902382-89-0

British Library Cataloguing-in-Publication Data. A
catalogue record for this book is available from the
British Library.

Typeset at The Poetry Business
Printed and bound by CPI Antony Rowe, Chippenham

Front cover design/photograph by Rob MacDonald
Author's photograph by Derek Adams

Distributed by Central Books Ltd., 99 Wallis Road,
London E9 5LN

The Poetry Business gratefully acknowledges the help
of Arts Council England.

CONTENTS

Lapse

Lip

Lip: Edge of cup, vessel, cavity, wound.

'Fie, fie upon her!
There's language in her eye, her cheek, her lip,
Nay, her foot speaks; her wanton spirits look out
At every joint and votive of her body.'

Troilus and Cressida, William Shakespeare

How It All Started

Do you know this dream? An exam room
full of neat, serious girls, your lucky gonk
by your fountain pen, the plop of tennis balls
through an open window. You're here for
'O' level history on The Causes
Of The First World War but you've no idea –
too busy bunking off to watch *Crown Court*,
and the teacher says *You may turn over*
and begin and there's a question
on the Algeciras crisis and all you can think is,
Algeciras sounds like a virus or a cloud formation,
your eyes blur, scanning for something
you understand, you wonder who Bismarck was,
why his web of Alliances was so significant,
your throat swells like a new loaf, you watch
the girls who know the answers to these things,
and you think of the stutter of gunfire, a soldier's
booted foot lying in a puddle, how the leather split,
how the rest of him wasn't there, just a stump
of bone, and if you'd learned how it all started,
you might have known how to prevent this.
You should have known how to prevent this.

Snakebite

(i.m. Helen Penfold, 1961-1999)

Things are looking up. We've
found a pub where the landlord,
convinced by my smooth lies, your

proper breasts, will serve us snakebite.
He tips the lip of each pint glass,
froths in lager, pours cider and asks

How much blackcurrant, ladies?
You smile at him, murmur *When* –
we love how his hands shake

as you take your change.
We gulp like seasoned drinkers,
avoiding the stares of the old gits

with their bitter, their racing pages.
The drink hits the spot and
everything is funny. You nearly

take my eye out playing darts.
And at the Rec on the way home,
full of sugar and gas, we slump

on the swings we dared each other
to leap from as kids, jewelling
our palms and knees with grit.

We lean back under the night sky,
under all the stars we can't name,
we're full of how we'll leave

this dump of a town first chance we get –
how we despise the regular lawns,
the sagging paddling pools, we're

singing as we approach our road.
Today was hot, like the days,
buckling with laughter, we shoved

each other over on your drive,
the tarmac sucked at our sandals
and the ice-cream van played 'Lara'

from *Dr. Zhivago*, too slow. Tomorrow
we'll feel sick as dogs. But tonight,
here, under a bright, full moon,

we're amazing, and as we hug
on my doorstep, I taste you,
kiss the snakebite off your lips.

Losing It To David Cassidy

That hot evening, all through our clumsy fuck,
David smiled down from the wall. His ironed hair,
American teeth. Eyes on me, his best girl.

And his fingers didn't smell of smoke, he didn't
nudge me onto my back, like you did, grunting
as he unzipped my jeans, complaining

you're so bony, and demanding, *Now you do something –*
hold it like this. David took my virginity
in a room filled with white roses, having smoothed

the sheets himself, slotted 'How Can I Be Sure?'
into the tape machine. And when we were done
he didn't roll off, zip up and slouch downstairs

to watch the end of *Match of the Day* with my brother,
oh no, not David. He washed me, patted me dry
with fat blue towels, his eyes brimful of tears.

Smoking and Reading Nietszche in the Kardomah

You're where I left you twenty years ago –
steamed-up café, formica, coffee-slopped,
a moustache of frothed milk on your top lip.

You'd like to have it sorted, as you frown,
still grappling with the Ubermensch, and so
hung-over from a night on Thunderbird,

make-up all smudged, your mouth a sour mess.
Your loose roll-up unravels as you suck –
strands of tobacco sticking to your tongue

like bitter little scraps of clever talk.
You never got the hang of it, did you? –
not smoking, which you hoped would make you cool

but only ever made you cough – and not
the Will to Power, however hard you tried.
You couldn't grasp that huge exuberance –

that what you had to do was say *I'm great*
and stuff the rest of you. You were too scared,
too shy to raise your chin and stride on stage.

So – gulp the lukewarm dregs and stub the tab;
now wipe your mouth and pack away your book.
Your blood-sugar is low. Try not to shake.

Outside the rain is sliding down the glass,
the pavements gleam, the buses squelch and spray.
Get ready for the years of screwing up –

the nights with men who won't remember you,
a shadow on your lungs, biding its time.
Nietzsche may be some help. Goodbye. Good luck.

Stitches

Relax, this is the first bit, says Tim,
your named nurse, *the local anaesthetic.*
The light in your face is blinding,
the syringe slides in just below
the eyebrow, on the bone.
His forehead gleams as he cups your cheek
as gently as a lover and says
Stay still for me now, this will sting a little –
shit, a little! – you can feel
the lonely heat of the needle,
the nerve endings fizz and jump
with sudden pain – you watch this man
with his tender fingers who numbs you first,
then flashes blue nylon centimetres
from your eye, this kind stranger you trust
to stitch your wound. You close your eyes
and try to drift, but think instead
of the last time you lay in this hospital –
level thirteen, your new boy's sticky head
blissed out on your nipple, the light between
your stirruped legs, your knees
distant white moons and a doctor
patiently sewing you back together –
the deft flick of her wrists, her murmuring
Nearly there now, when you flinched.

Fontanelle

It throbbed like a slow naked heart, the soft
part of you your skull hadn't welcomed
in its cradle of bone. I poured water
over your strips of old-man's hair
hardly daring to touch it.

Sixteen years on I watch you
header footballs into a net,
and with each rush of air, each thump,
feel the weight of your head again, hear
the midwife's voice – *Be careful of that bit.*

Milk

All it took was a stranger's baby
mewling in the supermarket –
the thin wail that throws a switch
inside the body, an unleashing,
and my breasts tingled and filled.
My son was at home, between feeds –
his mouth, no doubt, already puckered
while his grandparents dozed
over their papers. I stood in the aisle
clutching cereal, a slow heat
rising through my breasts, shame
like a dream of public nakedness.
And then the milk leaked –
soaked my cotton shirt,
the blue-tinged milk he sniffed out,
rooted for, the life force I was wasting.
I folded my arms across my chest,
my wet patches, as guilty as if,
my body programmed to release
this sweet, illicit flood, I'd seen
an ex lover, and suddenly come.

Back

If you go back, the kitchen will be
full of green water, you'll hear
the slow gulp as it swallows the table and chairs,
there'll be a dance of colanders,
wooden spoons. Upstairs
on the bathroom floor, the mermaid
will be dead, a husk of herself,
her poor scales dried to psoriasis,
and in your old room the cat
will squeeze blind, sticky kittens
into a box, where they will starve,
while the rats in the attic
grow to the size of Jack Russells. Even
the King-size marble with the
turquoise spiral will have smashed
falling from a shelf one wild night; don't
go back. Don't go back. The waters
are rising, there's nothing there
for you, stay here with me. Let others
shutter the house, wrap it, tip it
off the edge of the world.

After Rain

the garden writhes with them – green jewels
              pulsing on the lawn, or slimed, prostrate,
over stones.
                    The patio shimmers,
a latex of rain-skin,
              and they materialise as though
the water's called them forth
              from seed. I open the back door,
watch them bloat and pulse,
the air sweet with wet soil,
                washed honeysuckle.

And when the sky clears, water soaks
              into the earth, as though it's never been.
They shrivel, return to their ponds,
              undersides of dripping hedges,
the sudden streams
              that spawned them.

Temperature

You shake it briskly, and together we watch
the mercury crawl towards its resting place –
38.5. I love this dangerous heat – the temperature
where my dreams are luminous, where I give
speeches in Parliament, naked, in fluent French,
or gut herring in an Aberdeen car-park, or lie
under pink clouds on a glass-smooth Italian lawn,
peacocks nipping at my clothes. And, awake,
this is the heat I need to remember other temperatures –
at 121, sugar turns to toffee, -273 is absolute zero
while at 600, steel glows red and at 0, ice melts.
And there's no good reason for knowing these things,
at this moment, deliciously glazed and spaced out
as I am – except they're all so beautiful – just the thought
of that ice, suddenly liquid, dripping through fingers! –
they're laws, they keep us safe. Don't they?
You damp-flannel my forehead. *I'm calling the doctor.*
Yes, call him, my love, call him. Let him be whiskered,
Victorian, with a fob-watch and the smell of camphor;
we'll watch him handle the thermometer reverently,
and his eyes will glitter, enchanted by the mercury.

Ascension

On 6th July 2005, a fifteen year old girl sleep-walked from her home in East Dulwich and was spotted at 2 a.m., curled fast asleep on the counterweight of a crane.

She doesn't register
the slap of pavement

underfoot
then the grip

of each rung
as she ascends

towards the sky –
a mild night,

stars winking
over the library,

the railway station,
the Curry Club.

She's not dreaming this,
she's not dreaming

anything. Something
drives her upwards –

to curl her body
on cooled steel

rest her cheek
against the dust

and pigeon shit,
unaware

she could roll off
like a pea on the blade

of a knife, and her
mouth opens,

bubbles spit,
her limbs still warm

from the tangled nest
of sheets –

she's not dreaming this,
she's not dreaming

anything, she's risen
above the tilt

of the earth,
she's risen

as high as she can,
as high as this.

Cut

We wake to silence, darkness –
as I open the kitchen door
the fridge-freezer's tight-lipped,
cheddar sweats in its plastic,
lettuce curls in on itself.
I lift a bag of waterlogged peas
sagging like a sleeping baby,
pork chops suddenly pink and fat again,
yielding to our fingers. You joke
we'll need to build an ice house
in the garden. The radio and TV
stay defiantly dumb, we try
the switches hourly. Their stiff clicks
give nothing back. But as
the days go on, and lights stay off,
we marvel at stars suddenly blazing
in a hectic sky over the dark city.
We leave one candle burning –
now our bodies are half lit, we're
ripely beautiful as Caravaggio paintings,
we can't get enough of each other.
We relish the deep, quiet nights,
salted meat. Tonight we sense snow
in the wind, wolves padding
through suburbs, closer to our heat.

Hero

We are all his loves, his sweethearts. He doesn't mind
when we don't have the right change, he beams, we feel
adored as we lug our bags, our kids, onto our laps.
He's philosophical about April's pounding rain, ice
in November. He croons 'Danny Boy' as he takes the third exit
onto the by-pass. He'd take us further if he could –
drive us down the Champs Elysées, to re-vamp our wardrobes,
he'd park the Stagecoach bus outside Prada or Luis Vuitton
while he checked the racing pages. He'd say *That jacket*
is just dandy with those jeans, my darling, you're a sight
for sore eyes, so you are. He'd happily divert to a vineyard
in the Dordogne despite the sticky heat, the engine panting
and ticking, wait patiently as we swilled, spat, exclaimed,
he'd help us heave our mixed-case boxes up the steps –
nothing too much trouble. He'd drive us through deserts,
stop the dusty 29 by Bedouin tents, as we squatted
on cumin-coloured sand, sipped mint tea with bright-eyed men
who'd like to be our husbands. It's only the timetable, we know,
that keeps him from obliging us – only the need to be back
in the depot for a brew, a bit of a craic with the lads,
otherwise, of course, he'd take us directly to our doors,
ease tight shoes from feet no longer sore from dancing
and late-nights in back alleys, but from the tired lives
we've ended up with. He'd take the weight of our sadness
on his shoulders, bleed the radiators, put the kettle on, pull up
ground elder – but for now he winks, teases us into our seats,
eases into traffic, the rain-slicked road, the fading afternoon.

Your Unsalted Butter Is Still In My Fridge

behind my Cheddar, my ageing Red Leicester.
Your favourite brand, 'President';
plastered thick on baguettes, not a thought
for cholesterol. I could throw it out,
but won't. I might melt it
over minted new potatoes, to feed
a new lover. I'll find him in a gallery –
not Tate Britain, where I got you
that winter's afternoon, lips and fingers
numb, you slagging off Stanley Spencer.
I'll avoid the museum café where
you cut my muffin into four neat chunks,
the blueberries like blood clots. *The four
chambers of your heart*, you said,
(I thought you clever). You laughed
at me, the crumbs I made. No, not there.
I'll find my next lover at an exhibition
of English landscapes in Bond Street,
I'll get a quiet, unpretentious one and yes,
cook Sunday roast with all the trimmings
and when we've loved the afternoon away
I'll lick his flushed neck, taste the honest salt.

Eve To The Serpent

Stretched on tiptoes, knowing
your eyes are flickering over me –
at my sex especially – look
how I twist the stalk
and snap – pluck it carefully,
because it is precious,
unblemished, and wrong.
I've never been more curious
than this. I think about the skin,
how my teeth will rip into it,
about the flesh, how clean
and white it will be, how luscious.
You told me, didn't you? –
it will be the most delicious thing
I've ever put in my mouth,
its juice a drizzle of nectar.
It will do me so much good.
I might just stand here with it
in my hand, while you writhe
and sweat in your ornamental skin,
your tongue quivering. This could be
the longest afternoon of our lives.

The Visitors' Book At Gairloch

Alice, seven, has *enjoyed the pony-trekking*
while her mother notes *A golden eagle*
was sighted from our bedroom this morning,
a highlight of the holiday! They've seen
two whales, five porpoises. Their handwriting's
immaculate. Bill and Ida from Purley *found the rain*
depressing. I want to write that I saw a buoy
flare suddenly in the harbour, pink
as marigold gloves, or marzipan pigs
on a child's birthday cake, and the rain,
from sky grey as unwashed sheets,
is warm and peaty in my mouth; the air
here's so pure my lungs open like petals
each day, the water's so soft my hair
is stroked silk. I wake at first light, stretch,
and the skin on my breasts feels
twenty years younger. I almost write this:
The men who take visitors out in their boats
to spot elusive whales are all from Leeds,
know every seabird, every island, every ripple
and are the new gods in my dreams.
And I have such an appetite for lobster,
dressed crab, venison, raspberries, sex.

The Fathers

All over the city, women in restaurants,
cafes, bars, wait for their fathers.
The women sip coffee, or wine, pretend to read.
Some fathers arrive promptly, smiling –
dressed as policemen, or in flannel pyjamas.
Sometimes the father is a priest
in a cassock stained with candle wax.
One or two have pockets gritty with sand
from Cornish holidays. One father
flourishes a fledgling sparrow, damp
and frightened, from an ironed handkerchief.
One wears a taffeta dress, fishnets and stilettos,
rubs the stubble under his make-up.
They bring spaniels, Shetland ponies, anacondas,
they bring yellowed photographs
whose edges curl like wilting cabbages.
One father has blue ghosts of numbers
inked on his wrist. There are times the fathers
have been dead or absent for so long
the women hardly recognise them; some
talk rapidly in Polish or Greek and the women
shift on their chairs. A few sign cheques,
others blag a tenner. One smells of wood-shavings
and presents the woman with a dolls' house.
They might tell the women *You're getting fat*
or *Put some meat on your bones, girl.*
Some women leave arm in arm with their fathers,
huddled against the cold air, and window shop
for turquoise sequined slippers or angelfish
hanging like jewels in bright tanks. Others
part with a kiss that misses a cheek – lint
left on coats, and buttons done up wrong.

Colin Pepper I Luv U

It's painted neatly, white letters, next to
'Jesus Saves' and 'Liberation for Hunters' –
to think, a woman leaned over a bridge
on the M1, just north of Leicester –
maybe at midnight the week before Christmas,
her teeth aching in the freezing air –
declaring her love for Colin Pepper
to every passing motorist. Maybe
her oldest friend held the paint tin,
swigged neat whisky, told her she was nuts.
Was he worth it? Was he at home,
heating on full blast, fairy lights frenetic,
a tin of Stella cradled on his belly,
scratching his balls and waiting
for the big film on the porn channel,
while this enamoured woman risked
her neck? Or was Colin Pepper
wrapped up in donkey jacket and scarf
at the next bridge, facing Southbound,
his mate dangling him by the ankles,
painting his own message, his love,
under a night sky so cold and clear,
so full of unleashed snow, his face
burned, fingers barely able to grasp the brush –
thinking of how he'd warm her body later,
cover her breasts with kisses, the roar
and gulp of the motorway still ringing
in his ears? Perhaps in years to come
on Christmas Eve, both of them fatter,
credit cards maxed up, turkey in the fridge,
an avalanche of presents under the tree,
they'll toast each other, laugh until they ache,
and tell the kids about this night.

Original Residents

We're back, walking through the garden
while you sleep – tutting over your decking

and water feature, parting the leaves
of spiked plants bedded in shale,

where once, sore-backed, we dug for victory.
We miss the neat rows of cabbages,

the onions we flourished from the earth,
the white potatoes, pocked with eyes.

Inside, we brush against your clothes,
shocked you should need so many.

You don't sew, make do and mend, but heap
last year's shirts in black bags. Where are

your button jars, your slivers of saved soap?
Your radiators tick in the warm, still air.

We peel back your fat duvets. What soft skin,
we think, what soft, soft hands you have.

The Ewe

She came to us on a wild night, a steel wind
shaking the house to its bones. Snow
buckled trees, filled the ditches' throats.

We heard the door bang, found her
in the kitchen, chewing a dishcloth.
A beauty, my man said. *Not local,*

a black-faced Sussex yearling. She'd eyes
the colour of a drinker's piss, pupils
black slits. She stared at us straight.

Icicles in her coat, poor love, shivering,
and a reek of linseed about her.
She was no trouble to us;

did her business outside, like a dog,
followed me from room to room, toes
clattering like nails on glass. Watched

my breast in the baby's mouth, let him
tug her ears. She was like our own,
our creature; she smelled of herself,

her own wool, but also something of us –
our hair after rain. My milk; his sweat.
All winter she stayed close, barely bleating.

One evening as she lay by the fire, her belly
rising and sinking, her black lips smiling,
we joked she was dreaming of her own kind –

the press of bodies in the lee of a bush.
I held my cheek to her steady heart.
My man smoothed his hand over her flank.

And that night, I rode him, because he whispered
he wanted it that way; our eyes locked as he
lay under me, a tender, lovely beast.

We heard her panting before we saw her,
felt her soft, damp touch, lipping my arse,
snailing his thigh, and something in both of us

slipped its knot, broke free. He bit his tongue
so hard he bloodied his lips. *Stay there*,
he told me, *you stay there*. I watched him

drag her through the freezing night,
lift the latch on the out-house – closed
my eyes, imagining her gripped between

his knees. The neat slit in her throat,
the line of dark blood. Her dear, frantic legs.
It's done, he said, *enough meat to last us*.

Though she fills us, the chewing of her flesh
feels wrong, a sin. She's in my dreams
most nights. And my man reeks of her, still.

Night

We're moonlit, raw-eyed with insomnia –
the woman whose body bled away her child,
the man whose boss no longer meets his eyes,
the teenage boy still fizzing with desire.
We feel like freaks, we press our eyelids shut
and yearning for the sledgehammer of sleep
we count achievements, lies, commitments, sheep –
all useless. Let's stop fretting, and get up,

and gather in a street sugared with frost
then steal a minibus and drive for miles.
Let's all link hands under the glittering stars
and pity those for whom the night is lost.
We'll celebrate the earth's celestial hood
and greet the Great Bear, roaring in our blood.

Picnic

This way. He punches in the code;
five to midnight, the monitors glowing
like fish-tanks. The Veuve Cliquot
has roused them, their fingers
laced as he leads her to his manager's desk,
eases her clothes away like packaging,
kneels between her shaking legs.
She hardly murmurs even though
she's pressed against the in-tray –
this is an act of worship, but also unholy,
the desecration of the temple; the gods
will be angry with them forever.
Afterwards he asks *Are you hungry?*
They sit by the office fridge, and gorge
on Louise's strawberries, Geoff's garlic boursin,
Mary's half-bottle of Pinot Grigio.
They lick their fingers clean, kiss,
the cheese sweetening their breath.
She remembers her first picnic –
lemonade bubbles exploding in her mouth;
her mother's shoulders burned, thistles
pricking her through the wool blanket.
The songs in the long grass, swaying,
sandwich crusts curled in the heat
and the soft curdling of egg and cress.

Celery

You used to hate it – so pale and skinny-ribbed,
like the sleeve of a sensible light-weight sweater.
It contains so few calories you burn more energy
eating it than you take in. Bossy muscled women
in magazines order you to crunch it raw, steam it,
stir-fry it briskly. When you do, it tastes of water –
or of glum afternoons at your grandmother's flat,
the crack of it exploding rudely in your mouth.
It tastes of all those diets you went on
in your late teens, when you agonised
about your arse and thighs, when you adored
the minister's son, the engineering student,
the snake-hipped photographer who posed you
against railings on wet Saturday afternoons …
but today you read an article on boosting
sex-drive and find celery is wonderful,
that it stimulates the pituitary gland,
contains two pheromones that cause arousal!
All you need do is lie back, relax, snap a stalk,
shake off the water droplets, ease open the top button
of your jeans, stroke yourself and crunch,
wait for the chemicals to kick in, then ring
your lover on his mobile – bad timing, forbidden,
because he's currently standing by while his wife
blow-torches individual crème brulees for their guests –
and, with your mouth full of fibrous aphrodisiac,
ask him, *Hey, guess what I'm doing?*

The Biting Point

Thirty years dead and still curmudgeonly,
my grandfather is driving me through
the fog-numbed streets of Crystal Palace
at five a.m. He's in the plaid dressing gown
he wore to die in, and he's shaved,
badly, dark blood flecking his chin.
We're the only Austin 1100 on the road;
he crunches through the gears,
blaming the damp, bad oil, the years
it sat cobwebbed in the garage.
He slows for the lights, not best pleased
when the engine stalls – no part of his plan,
I know, to crank the key three times before
the damned thing fires – he's often told me
a good driver knows a car's temperament
like the back of his hand. As a milk float
toots behind us, he mutters, frowns,
eases one foot off the clutch as the other
trembles over the accelerator.
Listen to that! He's triumphant; the engine
warbles its surprise. *Like opera!*
That's known as the biting point, girl,
I'm just telling you so's when you get
a husband, you'll know what's what.
We coast down Fountain Drive; the car
sighs and dreams, a purring baby now.
He sits straight, sliding the wheel for a bend,
as the BBC transmitter sparkles
and winks in the distance – the last thing
he ever mentioned, the last fixed light.

Heckmondwike

This is his first afternoon with Madame
in her flat above the bookshop, the buses
whining through the drizzle along
Islington High Street. He likes
her colour scheme – bold purple, gold,
everything flickering in the candle-light,
very different from the magnolia anaglypta
and white skirting boards in Theydon Bois
– and the scarlet drapes and Turkish kilim
where a one-eyed ginger cat
regards Madame's whip phlegmatically
as she trails it across his thigh. He likes
the joss sticks dropping ash
onto the floor like insouciant students
though he's less keen on the actual pain –
the bite into the flesh; he slips further
from the room, each lash a descent
into darkness, his skin laid open,
vision blurring and that's when
he realises he's forgotten the Safe Word.
It's a place, yes – some northern town
he visited as a child. He remembers
grit-stone houses under a film of rain,
women in beige with bosoms big enough
to offer shelter and the smell of baking,
a wet dog itching its fur against his legs.
He'd said to Marjorie several times
he'd like to retire somewhere like that,
somewhere with hills, real hills, the light
on them blue as the day went. *Look,*
he whimpers to Madame, *do you think
you could stop that now* – but no,
she's in her stride, a real professional,

and he's so tightly bound, his wrists
chafing on her iron bedstead.
He can feel her breath on his neck, yeasty
and warm as the loaves in the bakery ovens,
swelling and rising to greet the new day.

After The Magical Realism Writing Workshop

You waddled out first, a half-grown swan,
still gawky and sullen in your dun feathers.
The woman from Bexhill-on-Sea streamed
out as a river of blood and a man whose name
I didn't catch split neatly down the middle,
argued with himself about who'd drive home.
The married couple left as ink blots, splodging
their way down stairs, while a young girl wept
as her hands grew transparent. Outside
we watched as black clouds leaked
overhead, streets bloated with dark rain.
Crocodiles raised gnarled heads, snapped
at gondolas, while the college broke loose
from its moorings, bobbed along the road
with its lights blazing, water slapping its walls,
and the caretaker – remember this? – refused
to leave, grabbing for purchase at door frames,
the captain going down with his ship.

Baptism

Sunday morning, nine a.m., we congregate
at our local pool. Almost naked, our bodies
hold no secrets from each other – like lovers,
we celebrate heavy legs, cellulite, fur, spider maps
of broken veins, ink blot bruises, the sad sag
of paunches. We know scars, birthmarks,
we've seen hair plastered to scalps, each body
poor and compromised. Underwater, it's as though
we're transparent – look through our glass skin
to our clotted hearts and lungs, our fat blue veins.
And yet the water parts for us, for our muscle
and sinew, blood and bone. I love the tattooed man,
a torpedo of inked flesh, who calls me *Babe*.
I want to stroke his mole-soft head –
damp suede – and tell him he's beautiful,
I love the way he swims, then to whisper
how cleansed I feel, afterwards, as we shower.

Sleep

Sleep comes reluctantly when you're in love –
a wilful child, still crunching leaves
in a cold garden, while the other kids
are inside having tea – sleep is not easily
fed and bathed and tucked in for the night.
Sleep slips from its bed and pads
from room to room, seeking out light,
sleep is thirsty at two a.m. and there's no point
demanding silence, showing it who's boss –
sleep will squirm and fidget in your arms,
whispering questions it shouldn't ask –
when next and *where* and *how?* – until,
at last, you kiss its eyelids closed,
its breathing slows, it sinks onto your chest.

Brother

This is the cupboard her brother
locked her in for hours
to keep her warm, and safe
from policemen, priests,
thunderstorms and boys;

where there's a brown mouse
who escaped the cat
and the hoover
and next door's girls,
the brown mouse she held
like a full purse in damp hands.

Where everything's her country
and every dress is a river
she can swim in
and every shoe's
a different type of boat;

and this is where she squats,
in the dreams where he's back
in her room, with the chocolate
and blindfold and his knowledge
of seven foreign words for *sister*.

Request

Send me your bed, but please, don't change the sheets.
Pay two strong men to load it on a van,
and drive it through the rain at one a.m.
I'll be awake, I need to search for stains;
let me caress your pillows, let me find
shed hairs, and place them on my tongue.
Then I'll lie back and, parting my damp legs,
remember you and me as we made love –

one last time – one last and perfect time.
We're better off apart – you, streets away,
mapping another's skin. Stay where you are
while what I'll touch is soiled. If you are kind
I'll ask for nothing more. Do this one thing.
I haven't slept for weeks. Send me your bed.

Fly

You lie in a strange room, on clean sheets,
aware of the urgent whine of his buzz –
the whirr and tick, the electric
tattoo he beats on the window. How,
you wonder, did he get in, squeeze
through sealed wood and glass?
His balletic legs are feathering the wall,
the bedside light excites him.
You're miserable now, this feels like
a broken vow – you promised yourself
you'd spend the night alone, but the fly
fizzes lust into your ears. He's
the two a.m. prickle of memories,
the soft insinuation of other rooms,
other sheets, knees nudged apart
after a skinful of Cabernet Sauvignon,
he's the lover jammed into your senses,
burned onto your synapses. He's filthy,
harbouring God knows what germs
and when your book slaps him flat
his body's a black smear, no obvious
blood, and a bit of translucent wing
flutters for a second, then doesn't.

Twin

A dark evening, and she's there
in the train window, her elbow
almost touching mine. I catch
her eye – she has better cheekbones,
fuller lips. As we stare
each other out,
the outside world rushes through her –
a lit-up family arguing over dinner
slice her chin and throat.
Her pen hovers over her notebook,
she seems preoccupied. As we slow
towards Clapham Junction
the other twins shift
and stretch – one man's mouth assures
his mobile he'll be home
in time to bath the kids, another's
head slumps into the night. When
we leave the train, they'll hang
in the black glass, and wait for us.

Bladderwrack

I shape your hair from dried bladderwrack –
black, unruly, from my side of the family –

hair like squid-ink tagliatelle. I crown you
with a twist of bright green rope,

press in lobster-claw eyebrows,
barnacled eyes, pink as a baby's cardigan,

and your mouth – your mouth's
a slashed-open razor-fish shell,

fish long gone. I necklace your throat
with ribbed white shells. Beautiful.

I build up the sand to give you
good cheekbones, think of the day

you'll come home at fifteen, a mermaid
tattooed on your thigh, triumphant because

you'd faked I.D. and anyway
the tattooist couldn't wait to get

his hands on you. That smooth flesh
singed, bright ink pooling beneath the skin

and nothing I could have said or done.
There's sand in your eyes now, your lips.

The tide's coming in. I leave you
on Gairloch beach, where the light

is hard and pure. The grey Minch
will come for you, sucking your hair

and face back into itself. It will take you apart,
daughter, beyond help, beyond saving.

The World Is Ending Pass The Vodka

(Paul Abbaszadeh)

The world is ending pass the vodka, pass it,
and make it finest quality Russian *Absolut*
in an un-smeared bottle with clear blue lettering

– pour me a generous measure and don't look
outside to see the buildings break and buckle
to their knees, fall face-first into the dust,

don't listen for gunfire and the crack of bone
or think of rivers aflame, or stained and bloody skies.
The world is ending pass the vodka – let's not

harbour daft notions of descent into the basement
with a radio, a tin opener and enough
baked beans to last five miserable weeks –

the world is ending pass the vodka, and as trees
crisp and shrivel, as soft drifts of debris
choke doorways, I'll try not to think of all

the places I never visited – the Hanging Gardens
of Babylon, the Pyramids, the sex club
in Rotherham for the over forties – let's say

Cheers! – we might as well have another,
let pure alcohol pour down our throats
and still feel a vestige of lust – so tell me, say

I was your best ever lover, hotter than lava,
the world is ending pass the vodka, say
you need to bang my brains out one last time

even as the ceiling splits, blesses us
with flakes of plaster, even as there's nothing
but the prospect of silence to drink to –

Lapse

Twelve poems

'We had fed the heart on fantasies
The heart's grown brutal from the fare.'

W.B. Yeats, 'Meditations in Time of Civil War',
no.6, 'The Stare's Nest by my Window.'

Blue Egg

That first morning, he boils her
an egg the colour of a spring sky,
a baby boy's first room.
She cups a hand over its heat.
It's miraculous, this egg,
conjured for her. He says
the colours vary – some
aren't really blue at all,
they're green as a winter sea.
Is there a God, she wonders,
whose imagination allows
the creation of eggs like these –
eggs so beautiful, and rare –
nothing a husband would serve his wife,
or a mother her child?
This love must be possible,
as he shears off the lid
and feeds her the first mouthful –
cloud albumen, sun yolk –
when eggs are the colours
of the sky and sea, when she
can kiss the hairs on the back
of his wrist and think of hens
easing blue eggs onto warm straw.

Crochet

Tell me something you did, she says,
when you were a kid. He says

he learned to crochet.
And loved it – loved the hook,

its sharp beak,
the bright wool,

unravelling like guts
in his mum's wicker basket.

A ridiculous thing for a boy,
in his dad's opinion,

to sit by a winter fire,
growing a blanket; but he

kept going. The pads of his fingers
hardened as he grew more skilled,

knowing soon it would cover his bed
like the sloughed-off pelt

of some extraordinary creature; how,
in the dark, he could fit his thumbs

into the holes. *I wanted to tell you,*
he says, *this thing I did,*

and lies her down,
frees her from her clothes.

She's cold, she breathes him in,
his salt, his sweat, and longs for

the warm prickle of wool
against her skin.

Metal

Because her belly's tender
and her shoulders ache
he lifts her into the bath
and soaps her breasts,
throat, arms and waits
until she's limp with pleasure,
then tips a jug of water
over her face, asks her
if she's ever wanted
a tail and fins.
When she splutters,
laughs, he lifts her
from the water, lays her
on fresh towels, and when
he presses his tongue
into her sex she gasps
and he looks up, says
she tastes like metal,
old coins, like swallowed water
from the brackish stream
where he and his brothers
swam and fished
when they were kids.

China

Her mother's birthday; fine china or glass
should do it. The shop's quiet as a chapel.
These are just in. The assistant guides her
to a flock of shepherdesses with flushed cheeks.

Her fingers brush the porcelain while
the Chinese eggs he'd bought for her birthday
start to stir. She thinks of him, lifting them tenderly
from their nest, two cool, creamy spheres

in his damp palm, and how he'd pushed them
inside her until they were snugly bedded,
– identical twins, joined by a knotted cord,
each harbouring a frisky jumping bean

and already they twitch and clack
like bare knuckles rapping wood,
as she bends to inspect glass swans,
a Caithness paperweight, bloodshot

as an eyeball. *Oh, God, no*, every small step
now brings her nearer to that moment
when she'll lose it, where she'll
cling to the desk and cry out.

Decorum, she tells herself, get a grip.
A shepherdess. Any one, she blurts,
stares at the woman's pale hands
laying the figure on its back, wrapping

layers and layers of white tissue,
she breathes slowly, listens to the rustle,
the crackle of paper and tape, she can hardly
open her bag to find her purse

as he explodes inside her.

Le Petit Mort

Each time he takes her – his hand
gloved inside, knuckling
until she can't breathe –
the bomb she'd felt ticking
explodes – another life goes;
her fingertips prised from the sill;
brake-cables severed; water,
food and oxygen withheld.

Seahorse

She dreams she's made him pregnant,
the point of no return; she squeezes an egg
into him. New life begins; a neat football
of opaque cells. It settles in his gut,
latches onto his blood supply.
His skin's green-tinged in smoky rooms,
coffee makes him retch. She traces the baby's
feet, knees, hands, rising under his belly,
the sudden drag of five miniature knuckles.
She rubs sweet almond oil into his shoulders,
cradles him when he wakes after dreams
of falling. His body's waiting to burst open,
for their miracle to leap from liquid, into air.

Sancerre

Eleven quid, he says, easing the cork,
not bad. You'll like this. And she does.
Everything about it. Being naked
on his bed at 2 p.m; that he's chilled it
thoroughly. She loves the moment
he twists his wrist and pours –
the languorous gulping – and that
the glass he hands her gleams.
He'd have washed it, earlier,
then polished with a clean cloth so it shone.
The wine hits her tongue – she gets
lime, rain, pine-needles, a hand
inching slowly up her thigh. He sips,
lost in his own appreciation,
puts the glass down, pulls
his tee-shirt over his head.
She sips, swells, loves the ease with which
he unzips, shimmies jeans and trunks
to his ankles, steps out, kicks them aside
like a teenager, his cock already hard.
He takes the glass from her hand,
kneels beside her and her mouth's
bone dry – thirsty now, she's so thirsty.

Succulents

She's surprised he has them
along his window-sill –
these relics
kept in draughty porches
by great aunts – Sunday
afternoons in Eastbourne,
angel cake and bagatelle.
She hates their dusty skin.

And afterwards, spunk drying,
on his thighs, he crosses
the room, pinches a fleshy leaf
between forefinger and thumb,
says, *There's something
magic about them, isn't there?
The way you hardly need
to water them.*

Simulacrum

She hopes when she's gone, and he's alone,
he'll smell her everywhere – her perfume
on his shirt, her sweat on the sheets.
She knows the flat still holds her – as though,
like a cat, she's rubbed against the furniture.
He'll drink black tea, aching for her mouth,
the heat of it, and, now, clearing the living room
he'll find her wine-glass, with the red simulacrum
of her lips – and remember exactly how full
the lipstick made them, how long he'd placed
his mouth on hers, the warm berry of the wine,
surely he'll put his lips to the shape and taste,
her mouth coming to life under his tongue.

Stubble

His stubble's so sharp, so keen –
every kiss a cat-scratch.

She rubs in unperfumed moisturiser,
looks down; her blushed skin.

Smooths palmfuls of body lotion
onto her breasts.

One afternoon she ran, a girl,
through a razed wheat field,

barefoot. The stropped stalks.
How she bled, limped home.

Never go without shoes, she'd been warned;
you never know what's there.

All night her feet had throbbed.
She'd let the tears come, then.

Tonight she trembles as her husband
parts her knees in the dark,

kisses her rasped thighs. Please
let him not feel the scratches

or taste the little pinpricks of blood
her lover raised; his signature on her flesh.

Lapse

The road's dark and wet and
as the camera flashes, she knows:
three points on her license,
sixty quid she'll have to pay,
the chance her husband
will get to the envelope first.
She checks her speed;
fifty two in a forty-mile zone,
fuck. What were you thinking?
And she won't say
how, earlier, before she'd
climbed into the car
to drive home, her lover
dried her as carefully
as a hunter cleans a rabbit,
wiped a smear of blood
from between her legs
and kissed the insides
of her thighs until
she arched her back,
buried her fingers in his hair,
cried out. She slows to a crawl
as she nears the lights,
thinks of the moment
she was caught –
the yellow dazzle,
the parting of her lips –
and wonders, if the photograph
ad captured her face,
not the back of her head,
would it have shown
she was still kissing him,
hardly driving at all?

Jasmine Tea

Are you full? Her lover pours jasmine tea
into her cup. She wants to touch
his sealed lips. Her tongue's scalded.

Four days, no messages. Five. Six.
She replays the loop of that last meal.
Jasmine flowers sour her mouth.

Food sits on her plate like unopened mail.
Aren't you hungry? asks her husband.
Are you sickening for something?

She wants to dream of sex, but dreams
instead of falling from a swing, spitting
mouthfuls of blood and teeth onto asphalt.

Six a.m. Raw light peels her eyelids open.
She stands in the garden and the spring air
bristles her face. Her head is full

of baby sparrows, screaming to be fed.